Harper,

I hope you enjoy reading this book and always remember to follow BUGS' rules.

Love,
Kimberly + BUGS
xo

BUGS BOODLE'S™

Book of Basics

by

Kimberly O'Hara

If you purchased this book without a cover you should be aware that this book is stolen property. It was reported as "unsold and destroyed" to the publisher and neither the author nor the publisher has received any payment for this "stripped book."

BUGS BOODLE'S BOOK OF BASICS

Copyright © 2011 by Kimberly O'Hara. All rights reserved, including the right to reproduce this book, or portions thereof, in any form. No part of this text may be reproduced, transmitted, downloaded, decompiled, reverse engineered, or stored in or introduced into any information storage and retrieval system, in any form or by any means, whether electronic or mechanical without the express written permission of the author. The scanning, uploading, and distribution of this book via the Internet or via any other means without the permission of the publisher is illegal and punishable by law. Please purchase only authorized electronic editions, and do not participate in or encourage electronic piracy of copyrighted materials.

The publisher does not have any control over and does not assume any responsibility for author or third-party websites or their content.

Cover Art and Illustrations by Jorge Pacheco

Visit the author's website
http://www.bugsboodle.com

Bugs Boodles™ is a Trademark of Kimberly O'Hara

Published by: Telemachus Press, LLC
Visit our website: http://www.telemachuspress.com

ISBN 978-1-937387-12-9 (Hardback)

Library of Congress Control Number: 2011939362

Version 2011.10.06

Printed in the United States of America
10 9 8 7 6 5 4 3 2 1

Dedication

To my wonderful husband, T.J., whose love I could not live without. And of course to "the Pack," Nikki, London, and Coco Chanel (aka Bugs Boodle) who love and snuggle me on every possible occasion.

In memory of Constance, Molly, and Wally, who would have been so happy to see this book published.

Foreword

(A special note to parents: you may wish to remove this page after reading)

Like most of us, children are naturally attracted to dogs. If they see a dog, they usually want to play with it or pet it. Unfortunately, their uninhibited excitement can occasionally place them in great jeopardy.

According to the most recently recorded statistics of the Center for Disease Control (CDC):
- More than 4.7 million people are bitten by dogs in the United States each year
- Approximately 900,000 of them require medical attention
- Over 1,000 people seek emergency medical treatment
- More than half of the injuries involve the facial area of the injured party
- Approximately 85 people per day require reconstructive surgery because of a dog bite, and
- 25 to 35 people lose their lives each year as the result of dog bites.

The cost of these attacks is also significant. They result in over $1 billion in economic losses each year. Insurance only covers about one-third of those loses. The remaining two-thirds are suffered out-of-pocket by the families.

This is not to suggest that dogs should be feared in any way. They are usually loving animals and *wonderful* pets. However, when treated poorly or approached improperly, *any* dog can pose a threat. This is particularly true with respect to children.

Children between the ages of 5 and 9 incur the highest incidence of severe dog bites that require medical attention (with 77% of the injuries occurring in the facial area). This is not because dogs target children, but rather because children are often ill prepared to interact with dogs.

That is the purpose of *Bugs Boodle's Book of Basics*; to teach children simple "rules" that will help keep them safe around family pets and other dogs that they will undoubtedly encounter. While children often don't retain the training we give them from our adult perspective, they *do* retain lessons that are communicated in a fun way (from *their* perspective) through rhyme and pictures.

Bugs Boodle's Book of Basics is designed to allow you to share in the experience. Please take the time to read it to your youngest children until such time that they can read it themselves. If it becomes a "favorite" of theirs, they are far more likely to remember to "do the right thing" when they interact with a family pet or are confronted with the temptation to approach a strange dog.

Together, with a little help from *Bugs Boodle*, we can make the world safer for the children *and* pets we love so dearly.

Introduction

There is a dog, who's named Bugs Boodle,
He's very smart and uses his noodle.

He has a toy that his Mom mends,
Named Teddy, the bear, that's his best friend.

Together they are two good boys,
Who share their time ... and sometimes toys.

They hope to teach you all they know,
About meeting puppies while on the go!

There are some things you need to know,
This book has rules that we can show.
So ask your parents if it's okay,
If you see a dog and you'd like to play.

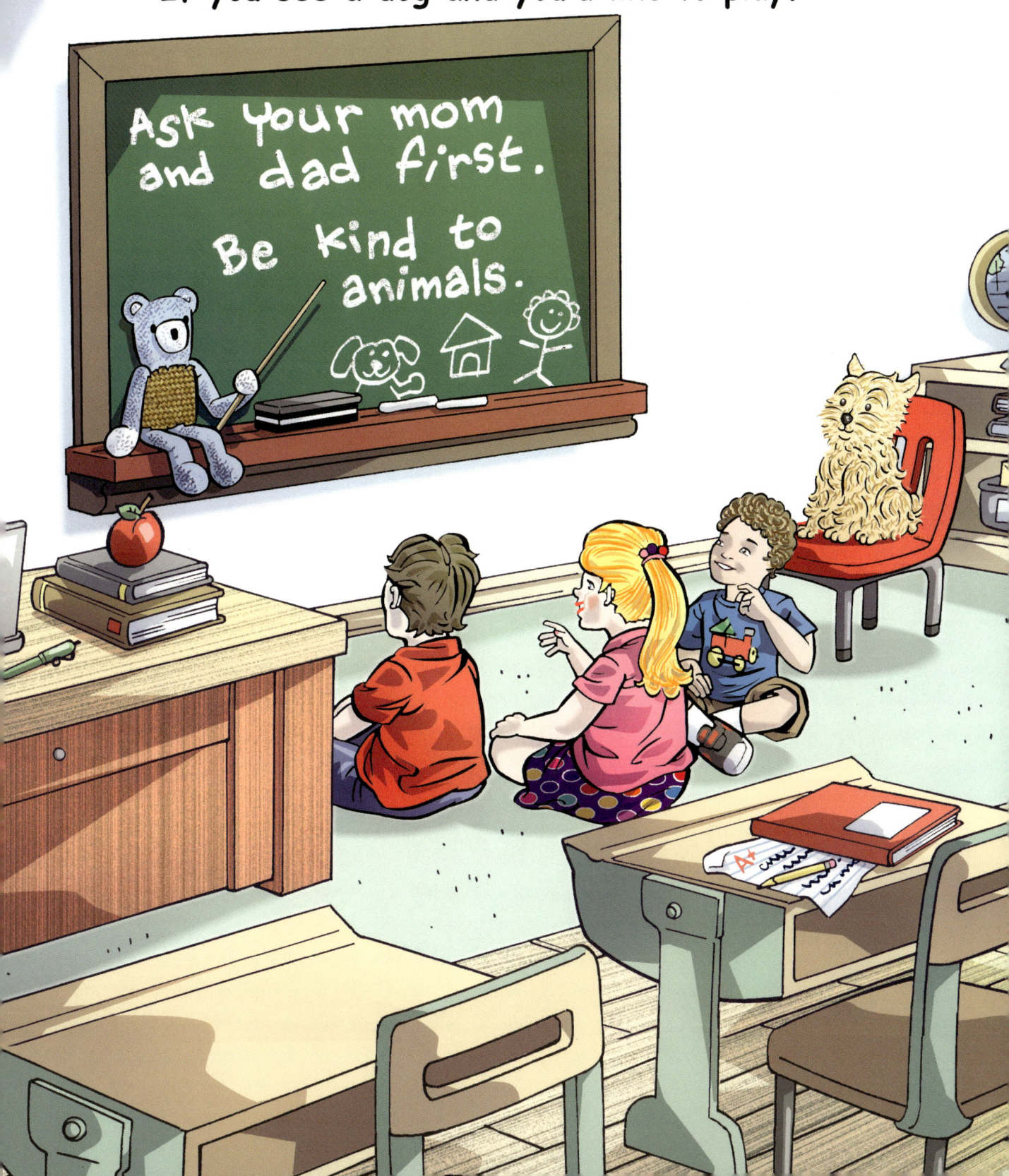

With floppy ears and wagging tails,
They like to run on hills and trails.

They have four feet that sometimes stink,
And so we scrub them in the sink.

They're snuggly, cuddly, snoodley, boodley,
Buggety, buggety, boo!

And that's what makes them oh so cute,
And want to chew your shoes.

Wagging tails are the way dogs show,
Who gets to pet them...and when THEY say NO!

Dogs' parents want to keep pets safe,
So make sure you ask first... and wait.

And when you come to pet their pup,
They want to know, you won't pet rough.

Moving fast can scare a pet,
Especially when they're soaking wet.

And whether they're a girl or boy,
They always have a favorite toy.

You want to ask before you throw,
Because the answer may be NO!

They're snuggly, cuddly, snoodley, boodley,
Buggety, buggety, boo!

And that's what makes them oh so cute,
And want to chew your shoes.

Dogs love to nap during day or night,
To wake them up would not be right.

Chewing bones can make dogs happy;
Taking his bone can make him snappy

Don't ride a dog like he's a pony,
It could hurt his back and make him lonely.

They're snuggly, cuddly, snoodley, boodley,
Buggety, buggety, boo!

And that's what makes them oh so cute,
And want to chew your shoes.

Dog's teeth are small and big and white,
And just like us they brush at night.

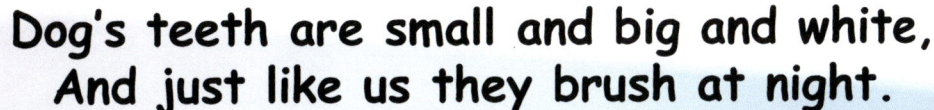

There are other tricks they like to do,
Like shake a paw and slobber too!

Pets should always have water and food,
To keep them in a happy mood.

They're snuggly, cuddly, snoodley, boodley,
Buggety, buggety, boo!

And yes, of course, you know it's true
They really do love you!

So ask your parents if it's okay,
If you see a dog and you'd like to play.

Epilogue

As an author, my goal is to protect children and animals from needless injury and abuse.

Hopefully, *Bugs Boodle's Book of Basics* will help children learn how to approach and play with animals in a safe and fun way. If Bugs Boodle can make children laugh while teaching them to respect their pets and recognize and report inappropriate behavior when they see it, he will have made the world a little better … for the children and the animals around them.

In that regard, we support the mission of the ASPCA (the American Society for the Prevention of Cruelty to Animals) and encourage you to do so as well.

The ASPCA was the first humane organization in the Western Hemisphere. Its mission, as stated by its founder, Henry Bergh, in 1866, is "to provide effective means for the prevention of cruelty to animals throughout the United States."

The ASPCA works to rescue animals from abuse, pass humane laws and share resources with shelters nationwide. Learn more about what they do, and join their fight today!

www.aspca.org

If you feel that Bugs Boodle has not only entertained your children, but protected them as well, please consider making a contribution to the ASPCA … and tell them that Bugs Boodle sent you! ☺

Best wishes,

Kimberly O'Hara … and Bugs Boodle!

About the Author

Kimberly O'Hara has spent years volunteering with charitable organizations that helped children and animals. She has donated considerable time and effort to causes that educate and protect children and care for domestic pets.

Kimberly provides a home to three loving dogs: Nikki (an Eskimo-Terrier mix), London (a Lhasa Apso), and Coco Chanel (a Yorkshire Terrier who serves as the inspiration for *Bugs Boodle*™). In observing many children's interaction with her own dogs, she recognized the need to help children better understand "right from wrong" when it comes to approaching and playing with dogs safely.

Kimberly created *Bugs Boodle* to connect with children at *their* level. The cute, cuddly pup and his best friend, Teddy, are designed to hold the attention of even the youngest of children. Kimberly also uses rhyme to help children remember the important lessons that are presented in a fun way. Her goals are to keep your children safe and protect your pets as well.

To see "what's new" in Bugs Boodle's world, please visit: www.BugsBoodle.com

About the Illustrator

Jorge Pacheco has been a professional Illustrator for over 25 years. He has illustrated a variety of children's books and has worked for almost every major comic book company in the world.

Jorge has been a staff artist for Harvey Comics/Entertainment and has drawn many famous licensed characters, such as *Casper the friendly Ghost*, *The Flintstones*, *Rocky* and *Bullwinkle*. He has also worked for Jim (*Garfield*) Davis and had his own syndicated cartoon strip, *CEO Dad*.

Beyond the world of cartoons, Jorge has worked on the design-side of JUNCO/Flamehead clothing. He currently works as an independent contractor and is available to create wonderful drawings and designs for you! For more information, please visit: www.pachecotoons.com.

Mr. Pacheco would like to dedicate his work in this book to Judith Ann Coan-Pacheco, his mother and a great lover of dogs.

CPSIA information can be obtained
at www.ICGtesting.com
Printed in the USA
LVIC080743100513
332955LV00002B